LOUIS XVII.

AND

ELEAZER WILLIAMS.

LOUIS XVII.

AND

Eleazar Williams.

Were they the Same Person?

BY

FRANCIS VINTON, S.T.D.

Reprinted from PUTNAM'S MAGAZINE

FOR THE

LONG ISLAND HISTORICAL SOCIETY.

1868.

LOUIS XVII. AND ELEAZER WILLIAMS.

WERE THEY REALLY THE SAME PERSON? *

BY the request of the Long Island Historical Society, I am induced to record the reasons of my belief that the late Rev. Eleazer Williams was "the Lost Prince," "the Dauphin," "the Louis XVII." of French history. I do not persuade myself that the following narrative will prove to be convincing to all readers; for, the problem, "Have we had a Bourbon among us?" is complex and recondite, admitting of no positive demonstration short of authentic records; which it may have been for the interest of various parties in France to suppress. Nevertheless, the facts which have constrained my judgment are too singular to be rejected as evidence, and may serve to confirm, in some measure, what has been written by the late Rev. Mr. Hanson, in the old *Putnam's Monthly* and in his two books, and by other writers less familiar to us, who have taken the same side of the question.

I. In the month of August, 1844, the Rev. Eleazer Williams, on his way to Boston, visited Newport, R. I., where I was some time rector, to ask aid for his missionary work among the Indians. He was the guest of Mrs. Com. O. H. Perry. Amid the books that covered the centre-table in the parlor of this hospitable mansion, were some volumes of French Revolutionary History, containing biographical sketches of notable persons, and illustrated by engravings of their portraits, in fine wood-cuts. These volumes were the gifts of Admiral Casey to Mrs. Perry, sent to her from Paris, after his return to France, in acknowledgment of her courtesy to him and to the officers of his squadron while lying in Newport Harbor. Admiral Casey, it will be remembered, commanded the ships which brought over the Prince de Joinville and his suite to America, about 1840, and remained at Newport while the Prince was engaged in his Western tour; during which he visited Williams with the surgeon of the fleet and his private secretary. The account of this interview is detailed by both parties, in Mr. Hanson's book on "The Lost Prince."

Candles had just been brought into the parlor of Mrs. Perry, when Williams and I drew nigh to the table to amuse ourselves for the hour. Not a word had been said of these books, nor of the conjecture (which was then a mere rumor) of the identity of Williams with the Dauphin; neither did I, at that time, entertain the slightest idea of any relationship between them. Williams had not spoken on the question, nor in any way alluded to it; neither did he know that the books on the centre-table were of the character described. But we drew near to the lights, by a natural impulse, to vary our occupation in a sort of "kill-time" way, and (I will confess it) to relieve myself from the task of entertaining a visitor who was commonly reserved and silent, and whose conversation at no time was particularly interesting and never instructive.

Thus we were engaged for a half-hour or so. I was reading some author, while Williams was turning over the

* This paper, received after our number for July was published, is a refutation—as unexpected as it is interesting—of the editorial note in that number, assuming that the theory of Mr. Williams' royal origin was finally disposed of and disproved by the article from his literary executor. It is proper for us to say here, plainly, that the present paper is written by the Rev. FRANCIS VINTON, S. T. D., assistant-minister of Trinity Church, N. Y.,—a gentleman whose high character as a clergyman and as a learned and logical investigator will command at once the most entire confidence in the impartial accuracy of his statements, and great respect for his conclusions—which so strongly lean toward the belief that Eleazer Williams was really Louis XVII. of France.—*Ed. Putnam's Mag.*

leaves of the volumes of the "French Revolutionary Annals." All at once I was startled by a sudden movement, and on looking up, I saw Williams sitting upright and stiff in his chair, his eyes fixed and wide open, his hands clenched on the table, his whole frame shaken and trembling, as if a paralysis had seized him. I thought it had. I exclaimed, "What is the matter?" and I rose quickly to rouse him; for no answer came. It was a minute or more before he could speak. But with great effort he raised his hand, and, pointing to one of the wood-cut portraits, at the bottom of the page, said, in a hollow voice and with great difficulty of utterance,

"That image has haunted me, day and night, as long as I can remember. 'Tis the horrid vision of my dreams. What is it? Who is it?"

I looked. There was no name on the page. On turning the leaf, I read that this number was the "Portrait of Simon," to whose care the Dauphin of France, son of Louis XVI. and Marie Antoinette, was committed in the prison of the Temple.

I shut the book; for while it was open Williams gazed at the picture as if fascinated, while overwhelmed with unutterable horror.

Some time elapsed before he recovered his equanimity. And then, for the first time, I talked with him on the rumor of his birth and parentage. He told me that the Prince de Joinville had visited him at Green Bay (as Mr. Hanson afterward related), and also that the surgeon (to whom, at his request, he had shown certain scars of scrofula upon the leg), said to him,

"*Mon Dieu!* you have rights which you know not of," and then suddenly checked himself.

Our conversation turned on the story of the Dauphin and on Williams' recollections of his own life. There was no assuming, on his part, of any other position than that of a gentleman (which he eminently was) who had been cast among Indians in early youth, and who had been educated above them in good schools, and who had done service to his country in the War of 1812; and, finally, had been called into the holy ministry of the Protestant Episcopal Church, and was now devoting himself to the welfare of those sons of the forest with whom his lot had been cast in early life, in the hope of promoting their civilization and their spiritual salvation, as their humble and contented missionary.

Williams assumed no other character than this, and rather seemed disturbed at the conjecture of his inheritance of any other name. There was no air of pretension—no attempt at speculation—no seeming personal interest in the matter suggested to him of his royal birth.

He could not account for his agitation at the sight of the portrait of "Simon;" and when I reopened the book at the page, he gazed at the picture without emotion, as if the spectre had been laid, and the associations with it had been buried and covered up in the mysterious tomb of the soul. Those wonderful memories, which the sudden apparition of Simon's portrait had revived, seemed to be mercifully remanded to their sepulchre. Williams retired to his chamber, and slept well. Meanwhile, we of the family, who had been conversing with him, puzzled ourselves with the explanation of the phenomenon of the evening, with as much satisfaction as puzzles generally afford.

But the conclusion to which my thoughts have arrived, after due consideration, is simply this, that *it was the Soul, through Memory, bearing witness to Itself, affirming the identity of Williams and the Dauphin.*

II. My next personal connection with the question of THE DAUPHIN happened in this wise:

The publication of Mr. Hanson's article in *Putnam's Monthly*, in February, 1853, occasioned many inquiries "when the Rev. Mr. Williams would again officiate in Grace Church, Brooklyn Heights." He had more than once done so, without remark; but now he was a celebrity. It was contrary to my principles and my taste to encourage the implied motive for attending divine worship, and I determined to gratify no prurient curiosity to see Mr. Williams while engaged in his ministerial office. On the first Sunday in February, 1853, I expected him to assist me in the Holy Communion; but I scrupulously withheld, even from every member of my family, any hint of my expectation. Indeed, Mr. Williams had failed me once before, and his promise at this time was conditional; so that I myself was not certain of his coming.

The organ had commenced, and the time was fully up, when Mr. Williams appeared, just as I was about to proceed from the vestry-room. He robed himself hastily in his surplice, and was directed to one of the stalls on the opposite side, which required him to walk across the choir, or chancel, of the church.

On the following Monday morning an esteemed parishioner, a German gentleman of high standing, called on me in my study to ask, "who he was that officiated with me on yesterday morning."

I replied that "it was the Rev. Eleazer Williams."

He then said that there happened to be in his pew, as his guest, His Royal Highness, Prince Paul William, Duke of Wurtemberg, cousin to the present King of Wurtemberg and to the Czar Nicholas, travelling in this country under the title of Gen. Count Heidenheim; who, when Mr. Williams walked across the chancel, asked my parishioner, Mr. R——, "Who is that? Who is that man? It is so! If there is any thing in family likeness, he is a Bourbon!"

Mr. R—— replied that he did not know who it was. But the Duke could not be quiet, but said, "It is so! He is a Bourbon! He is a Bourbon, *no doubt!* He is the image of Charles X."

Mr. R—— went on to relate the excitement of the Duke during the whole of the divine service; and how, at dinner that day, he resumed the theme, with many particulars in the story of the Dauphin.

Among these I recollect a few striking points, viz., that Charles X. was very like Louis XVI.;—that Prince Talleyrand knew all about the abduction of the Dauphin, which was connived at by the authorities of France; and when his Memoirs should be published (if there were no suppression of facts), the world would know of it too;—that the Jesuits knew all about it; and if Williams had been a Roman Catholic (supposing him to be the Dauphin), he would have been in France long ago;—that Robespierre and Count de Provence (afterward Louis XVIII.) were mutually interested in procuring the abduction of the Dauphin (inasmuch as he would not die a natural death under extreme cruelty): Robespierre, because he wished that the Revolution should maintain the reputation of a *political* revolution, and not be damaged by the imputation of being a war against children; the Count de Provence, because the Dauphin, as Louis XVII., would stand in the way of his succession to the crown; —that Chateaubriand would not take the oath of allegiance to Louis XVIII., on the ground that Louis XVII. was yet alive and in America; and that Chateaubriand's journey to America had for its object, among others, to discover the lost Dauphin;—that Count D'Artois (afterward Charles X.) would not swear allegiance to his brother until very late (when his own succession was in prospect), because of his scruples as a Legitimist, and his allegiance to his nephew.

These circumstances, and others quite as remarkable, were the disclosures of my friend Mr. R——, as having been the staple of the conversation of the Duke on that Sunday afternoon, after he had had a vision of Eleazer Williams.

The peculiar reason why this report was made to *me*, was this: A few days before this eventful Sunday, while I was engaged in reading Mr. Hanson's first article on the question of the Dauphin, Mr. R—— happened to call on me in my library. Our conversation turning to the subject, he denounced the article, and the credulity of those who entertained a belief in the "identity of Eleazer Williams and the Dauphin of France!" And his call on Monday morning was (as he states in a note now before me, dated March 3, 1853) "principally as a reason for retracting my previous unbelief, which I considered too rashly and too strongly expressed."

Mr. R—— wrote, in pencil, the title of the Duke on a slip of paper, and I made a note of some points of the conversation on the other side; where, also, I find it written, that "Mr. Edward H. Holbrook, of Boston, was present in my study, and heard Mr. R—— say the above."

The following is an exact copy of this memorandum:

*Copy of memorandum made on a slip of paper immediately after Mr. R—'s communication.**

"MONDAY, Feb. 7, 1853.

"Mr. R— gave me the address opposite" (side of the paper, in pencil,) "and said: The Duke testified yesterday to Mr. R— at his table at dinner, 'that the rumor was current' (interlined) 'Chateaubriand has said to him (the Duke) that the Dauphin was taken to America, and was now alive there.' When the Duke saw E. Williams in Grace Church, Brooklyn, yesterday, he said to Mr. R— (sitting in his pew), that Williams was a Bourbon, no doubt, if family features are evidence. The Duke has seen Louis XVIII. and Charles X., &c.

"Mr. Edward H. Holbrook, of Boston, was present in my study, and heard Mr. R— say the above, &c. F. V."

The address on the opposite side of the paper, given in pencil, is,

"His Royal Highness Prince Paul William, Duke of Wurtemberg, Gen. Count Heidenheim, cousin to Emperor Nicholas."

At this time there was no pledge of secrecy, as to this important communication; nor the apprehension of any harm to result from its contemporaneous publication. Accordingly, I took an early opportunity to acquaint Mr. Hanson with the general scope of it, and referred him to Mr. R—— for the particulars, to be printed in his forthcoming second article in *Putnam's Monthly*.

To my surprise, Mr. Hanson informed me that Mr. R—— declined to confirm what he had said in the presence of Mr. Holbrook and myself; for which reluctance he gave the following very excellent reasons, in a letter to me, dated

"—— Street, New York, March 3, 1853.

"Reverend and Dear Sir: With respect to the opinion of the Duke of Wurtemberg, in reference to the Rev. E. Williams, his explicit request to have his name kept out of any publication on the subject forbids me from complying with your request for a written statement of such opinion, further than simply to say, that the Duke, when seeing the Rev. E. Williams assist you in the services of your church, on the first Sunday in February, was very much struck with the marked Bourbon features and the general appearance of the reverend gentleman.

"And for the above-mentioned reason, I shall much prefer that, even to this simple fact, no allusion should be made in any publication. What I stated verbally to you, and to Mr. W— (his particular friend), was meant for a confidential communication, and principally for the reason for retracting my previous unbelief, which I considered too rashly and too strongly expressed.

"I cannot omit, however, to rectify a misapprehension which seems to have been created by that confidential communication, viz., that the Duke had heard from the late *Mr. Chateaubriand himself* that the Dauphin had been sent to this country, &c. This, as far as I know, was *not* the case. In short, the Duke spoke more of *reports* and *rumors*, than of *facts*.

"With great respect and esteem,

"Yours, R—."

On further consultation I learned that the contemporaneous publication of this testimony (such as it is) "would very much compromise the Duke on his return to Europe among the Legitimist circles of royalty." I reported to Mr. Hanson that the information with which I had thought to furnish him could not properly be included in his new article. But, forasmuch as I had revealed the particulars of the Duke's impulsive testimony, and my informant was reluctant to stand by me (for very good present reasons), I thought it just that at least the *substance* of what he had said should be confirmed by my informant, *in writing;* both for my own satisfaction and justification and for the truth of history, whenever the time should come to publish it.

My informant conceded the justice of

* I have carefully compared this with the original memorandum, and it agrees exactly, except in one thing, the full name of Mr. R.—*G. P. P.*

this demand with characteristic courtesy, only requiring that the document should not be used publicly, nor printed while the parties concerned are living, but kept among my private documents, as among my curiosities of history.

The following is an exact copy of the memorandum:

(COPY.)

"*Memorandum* for Preservation.

"In *Putnam's Monthly Review* for February, 1853, is an article by the Rev. J. H. Hanson, entitled, 'Is there a Bourbon amongst us?' in which the writer attempts to identify the Rev. Eleazer Williams, Deacon in the Prot. Epis. Church, with the Dauphin, Louis XVII.

"This article is causing much speculation, and has created no little interest among intelligent people, both here and in Europe. Mr. Hanson is to continue the inquiry in *Putnam* of April.

"On the first Sunday in February (Feb. 6, 1853), the Rev. E. Williams assisted me in the Holy Communion. His Royal Highness, Prince Paul William, Duke of Wurtemberg, cousin to the *present king of Wurtemberg and to* [this was interlined by Mr. R.] Czar Nicholas (now travelling in this country under the title of Gen. Count Heidenheim), chanced to be in Grace Church, Brooklyn Heights, that morning, in the pew of his friend R—, Esq. my parishioner, who, on the following day, informed me of the following particulars: On seeing Rev. Mr. Williams, His Royal Highness said to his friend with emphasis, 'It is so—that's a Bourbon, no doubt.' And afterwards, in conversation, at the house of Mr. R—, the Duke added, that Mr. Williams' resemblance to and general appearance with Charles X. is more striking than his likeness to Louis XVIII., who was less like Louis XVI.

"His Royal Highness had been acquainted with both Sovereigns. Furthermore, His Royal Highness on the same occasion stated that in the legitimist circles in France, he had heard it currently reported, that the Dauphin, Louis XVII., had been taken to America, and might be now alive there, and that Mr. Chateaubriand was conversant with the fact" [here follows a clause interpolated by Mr. R— in his own handwriting] *and taking all in all, he himself had no doubt, that the Rev. E. Williams was the Dauphin.*

"Mr. Hanson, having heard the rumor of this circumstantial evidence, has requested me by letter to communicate the above statement to him for publication in the April number of *Putnam's Monthly*, now in press.

"But as Mr. R— had informed me that His Royal Highness earnestly deprecated being in print on this subject, I could not gratify Mr. Hanson without conferring with Mr. R—.

"R— declines to permit the statement above to be printed, while the parties concerned are living, on the sufficient ground of the reluctance of His Royal Highness, and on the consideration that much of it was made in the freedom and confidence of his domestic fireside. But as the statement is valuable and worth preserving, I have submitted it to Mr. R— for his confirmation, to be kept by me among my curiosities of history.

(Signed,) "F. V.

"*Brooklyn, March* 5, 1853."

Mr. R—'s Confirmation is as follows.

"——Street, Brooklyn,
"March 5, 1853.

"At the Rev. Dr. V—'s request, I herewith confirm the preceding statement, on the first two pages of this sheet (of which this is the third), as substantially correct. The Duke of Wurtemberg was in the pew, No. 100, when he saw the Rev. E. Williams in the chancel, at the distance of about sixty feet.

"I cannot forbear, however, to add, that the Duke, being of rather an impulsive and sanguine temper, may have used, in the conversation alluded to, much stronger language than he would have been willing to subscribe to in writing: for it is obvious that, under the circumstances, the conclusion of the Rev. E. Williams being *no doubt* the Dauphin, or even a Bourbon, would have been extremely rash.

(Signed,) "R—."

"P. S.—It is distinctly understood that *no other use* is to be made of this paper, than that it is to be kept by Dr. V— among his private documents; as only on that condition I was induced to confirm, in writing, statements that were made under the injunction, if not of *strict privacy*, but certainly of avoiding a general publicity. A— R—."*

I have preserved this documentary evidence for fifteen years, as "a curiosity of history." But the time is come to publish it. In that short period of time Mr. Williams has died, the Duke of Wurtemberg has died, the kingdom of Wurtemberg is abolished, and public faith in legitimate kings is dead and buried. And, even while I am writing this article (intended, originally, for the Long Island Historical Society), the July number of *Putnam's* (revived) *Magazine* contains a paper of Mr. Williams' literary executor, entitled, "The Last of the Bourbon Story;" while the edit-

* I have carefully verified the above by the original paper, in the handwriting of Dr. Vinton and of Mr. R—. The only difference is the omission, in the copy, of the full name of Mr. R—.—*G. P. P.*

or, in his "Monthly Chronicle," begs pardon of the public for having yielded to "the enthusiastic faith and trust of the Rev. John H. Hanson, whose belief in the rightfulness of Mr. Williams' claim, and whose zeal in pushing it, amounted almost to a monomania."

Alas! dear brother! the world thinks thee dead, and bemoans thy credulity, while it is forced to honor thy "enthusiastic faith and trust."

But thou art not dead, but sleepest; and I, in venturing to indite *more* "last words of the Bourbon story," may be likened to that loving sister of whom it was said, "She goeth unto the grave to weep there." But that grave was the theatre of a resurrection. It was "THE TRUTH" who said, "Our friend Lazarus sleepeth; but I go, that I may awake him out of sleep."

III. In the summer of 1853, Mr. Hanson called on me in Brooklyn, where I was then settled, to acquaint me with what promised to be a singular confirmation of his theory, as published in the March and April numbers of the *Magazine*, through the testimony, he said, of Skenondough, a very old Indian chief of the Oneida tribe, who had known Williams when he was a boy of ten or twelve years of age, having been present when two Frenchmen gave him into the custody of the elder Williams, in 1795, at Ticonderoga; and who would testify that Eleazer Williams was of French birth, for the reason that *he had talked with him in the French language at that time*." Moreover, the old Indian affirmed that "Williams was *recorded in the census* of the Six Nations as a Frenchman adopted by the St. Regis tribe, and transferred to the Oneidas;" with many other particulars of great interest.

All this seemed, indeed, to be important testimony, if true. Who is this old Indian? How came he to turn up just at that time? What credentials does he show? What proof of his great age and sound memory exists?

These were among the queries that I thought proper to suggest, to guard myself from a credulity which I felt predisposing me to believe what the circumstance at Newport, some years previously, and the late testimony of the Duke of Wurtemberg, had fixed in my mind.

The answer to these inquiries was this simple explanation: Skenondough was a principal man of the Oneidas, who was accustomed to go to the city of Washington to receive the bounty-money, or on other business, of the Indians. On this year he left Syracuse with the usual contribution of Indian traps of bead-work, by the sale of which he paid his expenses. But there was such an unusual delay at Washington in the payment of the Indian annuity, that Skenondough's resources were exhausted. He was obliged to return without money, reaching Philadelphia penniless.

In this strait, he called on Mr. Peter Sken Smith, of Philadelphia, a well-known, wealthy, and highly-respected citizen; whose middle name was derived, I was told, from that of the chiefs of the Oneidas—"Skenondough,"—with whom the ancestors of Mr. Smith were familiar in their early settlements around Syracuse. Mr. Gerrit Smith, brother of Peter Sken, is, I believe, still the possessor of the immense patrimony derived from an Indian title.

Old Skenondough was hospitably entertained by Mr. Peter Sken Smith in Philadelphia. It was just at this time that Mr. Hanson's discussion of the question of Eleazer Williams' identity with the Dauphin of France was engaging the public mind. Mr. Smith, therefore, seized the opportunity of questioning old Skenondough on the subject. Skenondough had not heard of the theme, nor had he ever suspected that Williams was of *royal* blood; but he said that he knew he was a Frenchman, because he was present at Lake George in 1795, when he was brought over and committed into the custody of Thomas Williams; and further words to like effect, as above narrated, and as afterward embodied in an affidavit.

Mr. Smith thought it worth while to

acquaint the Rev. Mr. Hanson with this startling and unexpected confirmation of his theory, and suggested that Skenondough be asked to take New York in his route home to Syracuse, so that his testimony might be taken before a notary.

Mr. Hanson invited Skenondough to visit New York, where, by a happy conjuncture, Williams was also sojourning, while engaged in the printing of his "Indian Prayer-Book."

Mr. Hanson desired me to be present with him when Skenondough's affidavit would be made. I consented. Whereupon, on the day of Skenondough's arrival, I was summoned to meet the parties in the office of Richard Busteed, Esq., in William-street. There sat old Skenondough, his long white hair streaming on his shoulders, the deep wrinkles furrowing his swarthy face, but his form hardly yielding to the pressure of years. Mr. Hanson was by his side. In a few minutes Eleazer Williams entered; and it was impressive to observe the greeting of these old men. They spoke together in the Indian dialect for some time, then in English, then again in Indian, just as the subject of their discourse seemed to prompt. They had not seen one another for a long period; and reminiscences seemed to start up in rapid succession, while various emotions were evinced to the observer by their varying expressions of countenance—now sad, now merry, and now dubious, as if the recollections of one perplexed the other.

I watched this converse of mingled languages and pantomime, till I feared that the long summer afternoon would wear away, unless we went to business. Whereupon Skenondough settled himself, and related his story, beginning at the year 1795, when he first saw Williams and talked French with him—a "fou boy," as he said; thence he pursued the story to the time when this boy dove into Lake George, and was taken out of the water half-drowned, and carried into Williams' wigwam on the shore—after which event he recovered his reason; thence he narrated Williams' career through the War of 1812, and spoke of the Indian spy-system, in which the old chief was engaged—and especially referred to an occasion when they went together to obtain a subsidy from the United States Government; at which point, Williams, who had been listening attentively, as to a revelation of by-gone times, interrupted Skenondough, saying, "No; it was the State of New York who gave the subsidy;" and after some discussion whether it was the State of New York or the General Government, or jointly, Skenondough, as if tired of this question, exclaimed to us, "Let that go. He is not an Indian! He was never reckoned as an Indian. Look here! Look at his hand!" (taking it). "This is not an Indian's hand! Look at mine! It is double-jointed;" and so he threw his fingers "out of joint," backward and forward.

I mention these incidents, not as proving much on the main question, but because they happened; throwing, I thought, an aspect of simple sincerity on the intercourse of these simple but dissimilar old men.

I recollect asking Skenondough of his age. He replied, jocosely,

"I am old enough to be in my second childhood, as they say; for, look here—I am getting a second set of double-teeth;" and he opened his mouth, and showed us, sure enough, a fresh set of molars, which, also, he made us touch with our fingers.

The substance of Skenondough's testimony was, finally, put to paper, subscribed and sworn to, as follows:

"John O'Brien, a half-breed Indian, otherwise known as Skenondough, deposes and says, that he resides in the town of Salina, Onondaga County, State of New York; that he is known to the Hon. P. Sken Smith, of Philadelphia, and to Gerrit Smith, Squire Johnson, Mayor Baldwin, and Lawyer Wood, of Syracuse; that he is now directly from Philadelphia, where he was taken sick on his way from Washington, and is returning to Salina; that he is now very aged, having been born in Stockbridge, Mass., in 1752; that his father was an Irishman, of the name of Wm. O'Brien, and his mother an Indian woman of the Oneida tribe, named Mary

Skenondough; that, at the age of twelve years, he was sent from America to France, for his education, and remained there until during the War of the Revolution, when he returned, in the same ship with La Fayette, to America. After his return, this deponent went among the Oneida Indians, in the State of New York; and, in the year 1795, was at Ticonderoga, on Lake George.

"At that time, two Frenchmen came to the Indians on Lake George, and this deponent conversed with them, in their own language. Their names deponent does not remember. They had with them a boy, which this deponent supposed to be between ten and twelve years of age. This boy, the deponent talked with in the French language. The two Frenchmen told this deponent that the boy was French, by birth. The boy seemed weak and sickly, and his mind was wandering, so that he seemed rather silly.

"This child, after the Frenchmen had departed, this deponent saw in the family of Thomas Williams, an Indian, where the child lived. This deponent further recollects that he was at Lake George some time after this, when this boy, playing with other children, fell, or threw himself, from a rock into the Lake, and was taken out with a wound, he thinks upon the head, and was carried into the hut of Thomas Williams. After this he from time to time saw the boy, and that boy is the person now known as the Rev. Eleazer Williams.

"Deponent further declares, that, in 1815, when Mr. Williams first came to Oneida Castle to preach to the Indians, deponent was there, and asked Mr. Williams if he remembered his fall into the Lake; which he did not. Deponent further declares, that one of the two Frenchmen who brought the child to Lake George seemed to have the appearance of a priest of the Church of Rome. Deponent recollects Colonel Lewis, Captain Peters, Captain Jacob Francis, chiefs of the St. Regis tribe, who always believed Mr. Williams to be a Frenchman.

"This deponent also declares, that he was acquainted with Thomas Williams, and Mary Ann his wife, and that there is no resemblance between the Rev. Eleazer Williams and the said Thomas Williams, or his wife, or any of the children of the said Thomas Williams and his wife Mary Ann, who was also known to this deponent.

"This deponent also further declares, that Captain Jasper Parish, of Canandaigua, was appointed, by the General or State Government, agent for the Six Nations, some time before the War of 1812; and after the war was over, in 1815, he took the census of each family, for the purpose of distributing the presents from the Government. Eleazer Williams was set down by Captain Parish, on the record, as "*a Frenchman, adopted by the St. Regis tribe, and transferred to the Oneidas.*" This deponent was, at the time, a member of the General Council of the Nation, serving in the capacity of Marshal, and gave, himself, the returns to Captain Parish; and this deponent has seen the record of the census; which record may probably be found at Canandaigua, by writing to Mr. Edward Parish aforesaid.

"This deponent further says, that he remembers the spot at which the child, now known as Eleazer, fell into the water, and that it was at the south end of Lake George, on the west side, not far from the old Fort.

"JOHN O'BRIEN."

"Sworn before me, this 14th day of June, 1853.

"RICHARD BUSTEED,
"*Commissioner of Deeds,*
"43 William Street, New York."

The review of this remarkable testimony revives the impression of its truth, which it made at the time. Williams sat as one who was hearing tidings that were new and strange. While old Skenondough was relating his early history, his jaw drooped, and his eyes were fixed on the relator with intense earnestness; but when the story reached his middle life, his attitude and expression were changed, and he uttered ejaculations, now and then, such as, "Yes!" "I remember." Especially when Skenondough testified that Captain Parish was appointed by the *General Government* as agent of the Six Nations, Williams interrupted, and said, that "Captain Parish was appointed by the *State of New York;*" whereupon there was a slight discussion, and Skenondough's testimony was amended, as above, by the dubious alternate. While rendering his testimony, the picturesque old Indian leaned on his staff, holding it between his legs, and gazing, as it were, into the deep past. But during the intervals, when Mr. Busteed was recording the important facts, the conversation turned on the most commonplace topics; such as "the weather," and "what Williams was in the city for," and "when Skenondough was to leave;" as if the mind demanded relief from its musings and its memories.

The Rev. Mr. Hanson's fine face brightened as the narrator proceeded, like one whose disputed conjectures were verified as truth. I was in the intellectual attitude of a critic, hardly a skeptic, yet requiring further confirmation of the credibility of the witness. I resolved on the spot, therefore, to ask for this confirmation. It occurred to me, also, to provide a lasting memorial of this interview, by requesting that both Skenondough and Williams would consent to the daguerreotyping of their likenesses so that other eyes than mine might picture these old men, and see the difference in their type of physiognomy.

Williams and Skenondough consented; and, by appointment, we proceeded to Brady's Gallery, where their likenesses were admirably taken. These pictures are deposited with the Long Island Historical Society.*

In pursuance of my desire to learn the credibility of old Skenondough, I addressed a letter, on the 18th of June, 1853, to the Hon. Peter Sken Smith, of Philadelphia; from whom I received the following reply:

"My dear Sir: I have been much indisposed, and not able to answer your letter of the 18th ult. till now, and I am still weak. I have known John O'Brien Skenondough, a half-breed Indian of the Oneida tribe, for thirty years and upwards. I suspect the "important testimony" from him, which you refer to, relates to the Rev. Mr. Williams.

"I hesitate not to say, Skenondough can be relied on. I also know much of Mr. Williams.

"In much haste, very truly and respectfully

"Yours,

"P. SKEN SMITH."

IV. About this time Mr. Williams was carrying through the press his revised edition of the "Book of Common Prayer," translated by him into the Mohawk and Iroquois languages, by the request of the Domestic Committee of the Board of Missions of the Protestant Episcopal Church. This work required his frequent, and sometimes prolonged, sojourn in New York.

It was during this period when Mr. Hanson called on me, to say that he had received a letter from Mrs. Com. Read, of New Orleans, acquainting him with a fact which he deemed decisive on the question of the identity of Eleazer Williams and the Dauphin Louis Charles. The letter stated that further information had been derived from the old person (Mrs. Margaret Deboit, whose affidavit, on another point, is published in "The Lost Prince," p. 430; Append., 475), who was some time in the household of Count de Provence and the Duchesse d'Angoulême. This information, he said, accorded with a letter from Madame Rambaud to the Duchesse D'Angoulême, lately brought to his notice. The substance of this fresh evidence was this: that, when Naundorf's claim to be the Dauphin was rejected by the Duchesse d'Angoulême, she had said that "*when her brother should be discovered, if he were yet alive, there would be found, on the back of his shoulder, the mark of the lancet in the shape of a crescent, which was made there by the surgeon, at the time of the inoculation of the Dauphin, for the purpose of identification.*" And the letter begged Mr. Hanson to see if such a mark was on the shoulder of Eleazer Williams.

I asked Mr. Hanson if he had examined into the case. He replied that he had; and the mark was there, and he wished me to verify it. He said, besides, that if he had not found the scar of identification, his opinion would likely have been upset; for he might not justly have disputed the evidence of this woman's testimony, since he himself had journeyed to New Orleans to procure her affidavit. Time might indeed have obliterated the wound; and this fresh testimony might be rejected as hearsay; yet, nevertheless, he had suffered trepidation in asking Mr. Williams to allow him to put his theory to the test; and when he had seen, with his own eyes, this remarkable confirmation of his faith, he could not doubt of the truth, and wished, as I had served him heretofore, that I would consent to bear witness to what I might also see.

I found myself in a very delicate position. It was to request an aged and venerable man to strip his back, that

---

* We have not considered it necessary to engrave them, but any one interested can see them at our office.—*Editor.*

I might subject him to a scrutiny; while, on the other hand, I might, by declining, leave my friend alone to bear the sarcasms tossed at him as a romancer and a credulous person. I consented. A day or two after,* Mr. Hanson was to have his infant-child baptized by the Rev. Dr. Hawks, in Calvary Church, New York. I promised to be present on that occasion, if possible. I arrived just after the administration of the Sacrament, when the parties were dispersing, and proceeded to the robing-room, where I found Mr. Williams (who had been sponsor to the child), and Mr. Hanson, awaiting.

I shall not forget this meeting, nor the dignified bearing of Mr. Williams. I was reluctant to proceed. Yet I ventured to say, "I hear that you bear a mark on your shoulder, such as is said to have been put on the Dauphin for his identification. Have you such a mark?"

Williams replied, with a smile,

"They tell me I have; but I have never seen it."

There was no elation, no symptom of triumph, no suggestion that this report of his "identification" had ruffled the serenity of his soul as a simple missionary to the Indians.

I inquired if he would "submit to my examination, not from idle curiosity, but from regard to the desire of the Rev. Mr. Hanson."

"Certainly," he replied; "I should be ungrateful to decline compliance with Mr. Hanson's desire."

Accordingly, Williams threw off his coat and vest, and allowed me to scrutinize the mysterious mark. The light of the robing-room was very dim. I could see the deep pit of the inoculation on the arm. I could not discern on the back of the shoulder any thing peculiar. Nor could Mr. Hanson. Williams preserved the same calm composure while we were discussing the matter.

"Will you step out into the church a moment? there is no one there," I suggested.

"If you wish it," said Mr. Williams.

I opened the door, and he followed me outside; when, turning his shoulder to the light, there was the cicatrix, in the shape of a crescent, three-fourths of an inch across, nearly obliterated, yet palpable and unmistakable. Hanson saw it again, and tears silently stole down his cheeks. It was proof positive to him, *now* that *he had found* THE LOST PRINCE. He grasped my hand. We said nothing, except my ejaculations, "The mark is there! I see it with my eyes! What does it mean? He must, indeed, be the Dauphin!"

Such was the *final* personal observation that fell to my lot, to test the truth of the question,

"*Were Louis XVII. and Eleazer Williams the same person?*"

---

* The record of the baptism above referred to is certified by Rev. W. D. Walker, assistant-minister of Calvary Church, as being in the register of that church, and as occurring June 14, 1853, Eleazer Williams being one of the sponsors.—*Editor Putnam's Magazine.*

www.ingramcontent.com/pod-product-compliance
Lightning Source LLC
LaVergne TN
LVHW020637110826
845149LV00004B/1245
* 9 7 8 1 4 1 8 1 9 0 9 6 5 *